*"But Jesus called them to him, saying,
'Let the children come to me, and do not hinder them,
for to such belongs the kingdom of God.'"*

LUKE 18:18

ISBN: 978-1-942796-17-6

PUBLISHED BY
Letcetera, Ltd.
www.LetceteraPublishing.com

"*There is only Christ, He is everything.*" — *Colossians 3:11*

Now I Lay Me Down to Sleep

A Treasury of Children's Prayers

Edited by

Kathryn McBride

Letcetera
PUBLISHING

CHICAGO

Contents

Morning Prayers

1.

Now I awake and see the light;
Lord, You have kept me through the night.
To You I lift my voice and pray
That You will keep me through the day.
If I should die before it's done,
O God, accept me through Your Son!
Amen.

2.

O help me, Lord, this day to be
Your own dear child and follow Thee;
And lead me, Savior, by the hand
Until I reach the heavenly land.
Amen.

3.

The morning bright
With rosy light
Has awakened me from my sleep;
Father, I own
Your love alone
Your little one does keep.

All through the day,
I humbly pray,
Be my Guard and Guide;
My sins forgive
And let me live,
Blessed Jesus, near Your side. *Amen.*

4.

Now I raise me up from sleep,
I thank the Lord who did me keep,
All through the night; and to Him pray
That He may keep me through the day.
All which for Jesus' sake, I say. *Amen.*

5.

O Lord, my God, to You I pray
While from my bed I rise
That all I do and all I say
Be pleasing to Your eyes. *Amen.*

6.

Jesus, Lord, to You I pray,
Guide and guard me through this day.
As the shepherd tends his sheep.
Lord, me safe from evil keep.
Keep my feet from every snare,
Keep me with Your watchful care.

All my little wants supply
If I live or if I die.
And when life, O Lord, is past,
Take me to Yourself at last. *Amen.*

7.

In the early morning,
With the sun's first rays.
All God's little children
Thank and pray and praise.

I, too, thanks would offer,
Jesus, Shepherd dear,
For Your tender pasture,
For Your guiding care.

And I would ask You,
Be with me this day,
So that I don't wander,
And into danger stray. *Amen.*

8.

For this new morning with its light,
For rest and shelter of the night,
For health and food, for love and friends.
For everything Your goodness sends,
We thank You, dearest Lord. *Amen.*

9.

I thank You, Lord, for sleep and rest,
For all the things that I love best,
Now guide me through another day
And bless my work and bless my play.
Lord, make me strong for noble ends,
Protect and bless my loving friends;
Of all mankind good Christians make.
All this I ask for Jesus' sake. *Amen.*

10.

Jesus, gentle Shepherd,
Bless Your lamb today;
Keep me in Your footsteps,
Never let me stray.
Guard me through the daytime.
Every hour, I pray;
Keep my feet from straying
From the narrow way. *Amen.*

11.

Keep my little tongue today,
Keep it gentle while I play;
Keep my hands from doing wrong.
Keep my feet the whole day long;
Keep me all, O Jesus mild,
Keep me ever Your dear child. *Amen.*

12.

Jesus, keep me all this day.
When at school and when at play;
May I do all things I ought,
May I hate each evil thought;
Help me love and trust in Thee
Now and through eternity. *Amen.*

13.

O dearest Lord protect me
And my dear parents graciously;
With Your strong arm be ever near
To brothers and to sisters dear.
And all our loved ones in the land,
Protect them with Your own right hand.
From sin defend and keep me free;
Help me a Christlike child to be. *Amen.*

14.

My Father, for another night
Of quiet sleep and rest.
For all the joys of morning light,
Your holy name be blest. *Amen.*

15.

Now with the newborn day I give
Myself anew to Thee,
That as You will, I may live,
And what You will, will be. *Amen.*

16.

Lord, for the mercies of this night
My humble thanks I pray
And unto You I give myself
Today and every day. *Amen.*

17.

Whatever I do, things great or small
Whatever I speak or frame.
Your glory may I seek in all,
And do all in Jesus' name.

My Father, for His sake I pray.
Your child accept and bless
And lead me by Your grace today
In paths of righteousness. *Amen.*

18.

Now, before I run to play,
Let me not forget to pray
To God who kept me through the night
And awoke me with the morning light.
Help me, Lord, to love You more
Than I ever loved before,
In my work and in my play
Be with me through the day. *Amen.*

19.

Lord, in the morning I start each day,
By taking a moment to bow and pray.
I start with thanks, and then give praise
For all Your kind and loving ways.

Today if sunshine turns to rain,
If a dark cloud brings some pain,
I won't doubt or hide in fear
For You, my God, are always near.

I will travel where You lead;
I will help my friends in need.
Where You send me I will go;
With Your help I'll learn and grow.

Hold my family in Your hands,
As we follow Your commands.
And I will keep You close in sight
Until I crawl in bed tonight. *Amen.*

20.

We thank You Lord, for happy hearts,
For rain and sunny weather.
We thank You, Lord, for this our food,
And that we are together.
Amen.

21.

God in heaven hear my prayer,
Keep me in Your loving care.
Be my guide in all I do,
Bless all those who love me too.
Amen.

22.

I thank You, my heavenly Father, through Jesus Christ,
Your dear Son, that You have kept me safe tonight from
all harm and danger; and I pray that You would keep
me today from sin and every evil, that all I do and all
I say may please You. For into Your hands I commit
myself, my body and my soul. Let Your holy angel stay
with me, that the wicked Foe may have no power
over me.
Amen.

Evening Prayers

23.

Savior, lay Your hand on me,
Bless me, and remember me. *Amen.*

24.

Now I lay me down to sleep;
I pray the Lord, my soul to keep.
If I should die before I wake.
I pray the Lord, my soul to take;
And this I ask in Jesus' name. *Amen.*

25.

Now I lay me down to sleep,
I pray the Lord my soul to keep
May angels watch me
through the night and
wake me with the morning light. *Amen.*

26.

Dear Father in heaven,
Look down from up above;
Bless my papa and my mama too,
And all of those I love.

May angels guard over
My slumbers, and when
The morning is breaking,
Awake me. *Amen.*

27.

Now the light has gone away;
Savior, listen while I pray.
Asking You to watch and keep
And to send me quiet sleep.

Jesus, Savior, wash away
All that has been wrong today;
Help me every day to be
Good and gentle, more like Thee.

Let my near and dear ones be
Always near and dear to Thee.
O bring me and all I love
To Your happy home above. *Amen.*

28.

In my little bed I lie:
Heavenly Father, hear my cry;
Lord, keep me through this night.
Bring me safely to morning light. *Amen.*

29.

The day is past and over,
All thanks, O Lord, to You!
O Jesus, keep me in Your sight
And save me through the coming night.
Amen.

30.

The day is done;
O God the Son,
Look down upon
Your little one!

O Light of Light,
Keep me this night,
And show around me
Your presence bright.

I need not fear
If You are near;
You are my Savior
Kind and dear. *Amen.*

31.

Forgive, my Lord, Your dear Son
For the naughty things that I have done.
So that with the world, myself, and Thee
I can sleep in peace where You may be. *Amen.*

32.

Watch over a little child tonight,
Blest Savior from above,
And keep me till the morning light
Within Your arms of love. *Amen.*

33.

Jesus, tender Shepherd, hear me:
Bless Your little child tonight;
Through the darkness please be near me,
And keep me safe till morning light.

All this day Your hand has led me,
And I thank You for Your care;
You have warmed me, clothed me, fed me;
Listen to my evening prayer.

May my sins be all forgiven;
Bless the friends I love so well;
Take me, Lord, at last to heaven.
Happy there with You to dwell. *Amen.*

34.

Abide with me! Fast falls the evening,
The darkness deepens; Lord, with me abide!
When other helpers fail and comforts flee,
Help of the helpless, O abide with me! *Amen.*

35.

Lord, send me sleep that I may live;
The wrongs I've done this day forgive.
Bless every deed and thought and word
I've rightly done, or said, or heard.
Bless relatives and friends always;
Teach all the world to watch and pray.
My thanks for all my blessings take
And hear my prayer for Jesus' sake.
Amen.

36.

Lord, I have passed another day
And come to thank You for Your care.
Forgive my faults in work or play
And listen to my evening prayer.
Your favor gives me daily bread
And friends, who all my wants supply:
And safely now I rest my head,
Preserved and guarded by Your eye.
Amen.

37.

At the close of every day,
Lord, to You I kneel and pray.
Look upon Your little child,
Look in love and mercy mild.
O forgive and wash away
All my naughtiness this day,
And both when I sleep and wake
Bless me for my Savior's sake. *Amen.*

38.

The toils of day are over;
I lift my heart to Thee
And ask that free from peril
The hours of night may be.
O Jesus, make their darkness light
And guard me through the coming night. *Amen.*

39.

All praise to You, my God, this night
For all the blessings of the light:
Keep me, O keep me, King of kings,
Beneath Your own almighty wings. *Amen.*

40.

O Lord God, I pray, for Christ's sake, forgive me
whatever I have done wrong today and keep me safe
all through the night while I am asleep. *Amen.*

41.

I fall asleep in Jesus' wounds,
There pardon for my sins abounds;
Yea, Jesus' blood and righteousness
My jewels are, my glorious dress,
Wherein before my God I'll stand
When I shall reach the heavenly land.
Amen.

42.

Father in heaven, hear my prayer
Bless me with thy loving care.
Be my guide in all I do
and bless all those who love me too.
Amen.

43.

Angel of God, my guardian dear,
to whom God's love commits me here;
Watch over me throughout the night,
keep me safe within Your sight.
Amen.

44.

Angels bless and angels keep
Angels guard me while I sleep
Bless my heart and bless my home
Bless my spirit as I roam
Guide and guard me through the night
and wake me with the morning's light.
Amen

45.

I hear no voice, I feel no touch,
I see no glory bright;
But yet I know that God is near,
In darkness as in light.
God watches ever by my side,
And hears my whispered prayer:
A God of love for a little child
Both night and day does care.
Amen

46.

Dear God most high, hear and bless
Thy beasts and singing birds:
And guard with tenderness
Small things that have no words.
Amen

47.

God made the sun,
And God made the trees,
God made the mountains,
And God made me.
Thank You God,
For the sun and the trees,
For making the mountains,
And for making me! *Amen*

48.

Father, we thank You for the night,
And for the pleasant morning light;
For rest and food and loving care,
And all that makes the day so fair.

Help us to do the things we should,
To be to others kind and good;
In all we do, in work or play,
To grow more loving every day. *Amen*

49.

Dear Heavenly Father from above,
Look down on *(names of children)* with love,
Please keep them in Your care,
And tonight hear their prayer. *Amen*

Table Prayers

BEFORE MEALS

50.

God is great and God is Good,
And we thank Him for our food;
By God's hand we must be fed,
Give us Lord, our daily bread.
Amen.

51.

God is great!
God is good!
Let us thank Him
For our food.
Amen.

52.

Be present at our table, Lord,
Be here and everywhere adored.
Your creatures bless and grant that we
May feast in paradise with Thee. *Amen.*

53.

Abba, Father, bless this food
For our everlasting good. *Amen.*

54.

Come, Lord Jesus, be our Guest
And let Your gifts to us be blest. *Amen.*

55.

O Bread of Life, from day to day
Be our Comfort, Food, and Stay.
Amen.

56.

Great God, Giver of all good,
Accept our praise and bless our food.
Grace, health, and strength to us afford
Through Jesus Christ, our blessed Lord.
Amen.

57.

Thank You for the world so sweet,
Thank You for the food we eat.
Thank You for the birds that sing,
Thank You God for everything. *Amen.*

58.

Jesus, bless what You have given,
Feed our souls with bread from heaven;
Guide and lead us all the way
In all that we may do and say. *Amen.*

59.

Lord God, heavenly Father, bless us and these gifts
which we receive from Your bountiful goodness,
through Jesus Christ, our Lord. *Amen.*

60.

The eyes of all wait upon You O Lord, and You give
them their meat in due season: You open Your hand
and satisfy the desire of every living thing. *Amen.*

61.

Grant us grace, O Lord, that, whether we eat or drink,
or whatever we do, we may do it all in Your name and
for Your glory. *Amen.*

62.

We thank You Lord, for happy hearts,
For rain and sunny weather.
We thank You, Lord, for this our food,
And that we are together. *Amen.*

AFTER MEALS

63.

Thanks, Lord Jesus! *Amen.*

64.

Thanks be to You, O God! *Amen.*

65.

The Lord is my Shepherd, I shall not want. *Amen.*

66.

We thank the Lord
For meat and drink
Through Jesus Christ. *Amen.*

67.

We thank You for these gifts, O Lord;
Please feed our souls, too, with Your Word. *Amen.*

68.

We thank You, dear Lord Jesus.
That You our Guest has been;
O be with us forever, Lord.
And save us from all sin. *Amen.*

69.

O give thanks unto the Lord, for He is good;
for His mercy endures forever. *Amen.*

70.

Bless the Lord, O my soul; and all that is within me
bless His holy name. Bless the Lord, O my soul, and
forget not all His benefits. *Amen.*

71.

Heavenly Father, accept our thanks for this and for all
Your blessings, through Jesus Christ. *Amen.*

72.

O God, who gives us all our food, make us thankful
and provide for all the needy, now and evermore.
Amen.

73.

Accept, O Lord, our thankful praises
For all Your goodness did bestow;
May it increase our faith and lead us
Our praise by godly lives to show,
That every deed and word may prove
We trust and own our Father's love.
Amen.

74.

We thank You, Lord God, heavenly Father, through
Jesus Christ, our Lord, for all Your gifts, who lives and
reigns forever and ever. *Amen.*

75.

O Lord, we thank You for our daily bread. May it
strengthen and revive our bodies! And we pray, that
You nourish our souls with Your heavenly grace,
through Jesus Christ, our Lord. *Amen.*

76.

The Lord is good to all, and His tender mercies are over
all His works. Bless the Lord, O my soul, and all that is
within me, bless His holy name. Bless the Lord, O my
soul, and forget not all His benefits. *Amen.*

Prayers in Sickness

77.

Lord, help me! *Amen.*

78.

Jesus, Redeemer, have mercy upon me! *Amen.*

79.

Tender Jesus, meek and mild,
Look on me, a little child;
Help me, if it is Your will,
To recover from all ill. *Amen.*

80.

I am weak, but You are strong.
Help me, O my God! *Amen.*

81.

Dear Father, help me believe that all things work
together for good to those who love You. *Amen.*

82.

O God, from whom all blessings flow,
I lift my heart to Thee;
In all my sorrows, conflicts, woes,
Dear Lord, remember me. *Amen.*

83.

Dear Father, Your child is sick. Look upon me in tender
mercy, and if it be Your will, raise me up and grant me
health and strength. *Amen.*

84.

Other refuge have I none;
Hangs my helpless soul on Thee:
Leave, ah! leave me not alone,
Still support and comfort me.
All my trust in You is stayed,
All my help from You I bring;
Cover my defenseless head
In the shadow of Your wing! *Amen.*

85.

Lord, gracious God, I cry to You,
Bless me with Your favor,
Forgive my sins, and let me live,
Your child remain forever.

You have redeemed me with Your blood,
You are my only God, in whom I trust.
In every need, You are my Savior. *Amen.*

86.

Nearer, my God, to You,
Nearer to You!
Even though it is a cross
That raises me;
Still all my song will be,
Nearer, my God, to You,
Nearer, my God, to You,
Nearer to You. *Amen.*

87.

Lord Jesus Christ, the greatest Doctor, I come to You
in my sickness. I pray that You look upon me in tender
mercy. Send Your guardian angel to watch over me and
soon make me well. *Amen.*

88.

Lord Jesus, look down from heaven upon my mother
(father, brother, sister) and soon make her *(him)* well
again. You can do all things! Hear my prayer!
Amen.

89.

Heavenly Father, it has pleased You to visit me with
sickness, I know that You are too kind and good to send
me anything but for my blessing. Help me to bear my
illness and grant that I may soon recover, through
Jesus Christ, my Lord and Savior. *Amen.*

90.

Angel of God, my Guardian dear,
To whom God's love commits me here;
Ever this day, be at my side
To light and guard
To rule and guide.

Birthday Prayers

91.

Holy Jesus, every day
Keep us in the narrow way,
And when earthly things are past,
Bring our ransomed souls at last
Where they need no star to guide.
Where no clouds Your glory hide. *Amen.*

92.

As a little child relies
On a care beyond his own;
He knows he's neither strong or wise,
And fears to step alone,
Let me with You abide
As my Father, Guard, and Guide!
Amen.

93.

Faithful Shepherd, feed me
In the pastures green;
Faithful Shepherd, lead me
Where Your steps are seen.

Hold me fast and guide me
In the narrow way;
So, with You beside me,
I will never stray.

Daily bring me nearer
To the heavenly shore;
May my faith grow clearer.
May I love You more and more!

Hallow every pleasure,
Every gift and pain;
You, Yourself, my Treasure.
Though nothing else I gain. *Amen.*

94.

We thank You, heavenly Father,
For every earthly good,
For life, and health, and clothing,
And for our daily food.

Give us hearts to thank You,
For every blessing sent,
And for whatever You send us
Make us be content. *Amen.*

95.

Holy Jesus, be my Light,
Shine upon my way;
Through this tempting, changing life
Lead me day by day. *Amen.*

96.

Lord, be my constant Guide,
Lead me all the way,
Until I reach Your home at last,
Nevermore to stray. *Amen.*

97.

O God, You are a faithful God,
A Fountain that always flows,
Without whom nothing is,
Who all good gifts bestows:
A pure and healthy frame
O give me and within
A conscience free from blame,
A soul unhurt by sin. *Amen.*

For School and Church

98.

Lord Jesus Christ, to us attend.
Your Holy Spirit to us send. *Amen.*

99.

Lord, teach us how to keep Your day
And lead and bless us all the way. *Amen.*

100.

Lord, open my heart to hear
And by Your Word to me come near;
Let me Your Word still pure retain,
Let me Your child and heir remain. *Amen.*

101.

Direct me now, O gracious Lord,
To hear Your Holy Word;
Assist Your minister to preach,
And let Your Holy Spirit teach,
And let eternal life be found
By all who hear the joyful sound. *Amen.*

102.

On what has now been sown
Your blessing, Lord, bestow;
The power is Yours alone
To make it spring and grow. *Amen.*

103.

Blessed Lord, let Your blessing go with me today and
grant that I may be obedient to my teachers and may
learn with pleasure whatever I am taught, to Your great
honor and glory. *Amen.*

104.

Almighty God, Your Word is cast
Like seed into the ground;
Now let the dew of heaven descend
And righteous fruits abound. *Amen.*

105.

O most gracious God, let me never forget the many
good things that I have heard this day; but let them
abide in my heart, so that I may amend my life, that I
may be able to give a good account of them to Jesus
Christ, our Lord and Savior, when He comes to judge
the world at the Last Day, for whose sake I ask all
blessings, and to whom be glory forever and ever!
Amen.

106.

May the grace of Christ, our Savior,
And the Father's boundless love,
With the Holy Spirit's favor,
Rest upon us from above.

May we abide in union
With each other and the Lord
And possess, in sweet communion,
Joys which earth cannot afford. *Amen.*

107.

O give me Samuel's ear,
The open ear, O Lord,
Alive and quick to hear
Each whisper of Your Word,
Like him to answer at Your call,
And to obey You first of all. *Amen.*

108.

Abide, my dear Redeemer,
Among us with Your Word
And always, now and forever
True peace and joy afford. *Amen.*

109.

God of Light and Truth,
thank You for giving me
a mind that can know
and a heart that can love.
Help me to keep learning every day of my life,
for all knowledge leads to You.
Let me be aware of Your presence
in all things and at all times.
Encourage me when work is difficult
and when I am tempted to give up;
encourage me when my brain seems slow
and the way forward is difficult.
Grant me the grace to put my mind to use
exploring the world You have created,
confident that in You there a wisdom
that is real. *Amen.*

110.

Dismiss me with Your blessing, Lord;
Help me to feed upon Your Word;
All that I've done wrong forgive
And let Your truth within me live. *Amen.*

111.

Now our sweet worship is over—
Singing, praying, teaching, hearing:
Let us gladly God adore
For His gracious strength and cheering.
Bless His name, who would save us,
For the rich feast He gave us.

Let our going out be blessed,
Bless our entrance in like measure;
Bless, O Lord, our work and rest,
Bless our bread, our sadness and pleasure;
Be in death Your blessing given,
And make us blessed heirs of heaven. *Amen.*

112.

My God, accept my heart this day
And make it always Thine,
That I from You no more may stray,
No more from You decline.

Anoint me with Your heavenly grace,
Adopt me for Your own,
That I may see Your glorious face
And worship at Your throne.

Let every thought and work and word
To You be ever given;
Then life shall be Your service, Lord,
And death the gate of heaven. *Amen.*

Christmas Prayers

113.

Let us all with happy voice
Praise the God of heaven,
Who, to bid our hearts rejoice,
His own Son has given.
Amen.

114.

O Lord Christ, our Savior dear,
Be ever near us;
Grant us now a glad New Year.
Amen, Jesus, hear us!
Amen.

115.

O Holy Child of Bethlehem,
Come down to us, we pray;
Cast out our sin and enter in.
Be born in us today. *Amen.*

116.

O welcome, little Christmas Guest,
Dear Jesus, from above;
Upon Your face, so pure and mild,
We see God's smile of love. *Amen.*

117.

Precious Babe of Bethlehem,
A gift of love to sinful men,
You, our Savior, Lord, and King—
May we all Your praises sing! *Amen.*

118.

Ah! dear Jesus, holy Child,
Make Yourself a bed, soft, undefiled,
Within my heart, that it may be
A quiet chamber kept for Thee. *Amen.*

119.

Lord, this is my prayer
Not only on Christmas Day
But until I see You face to face
May I live my life this way:

Just like the baby Jesus
I ever hope to be,
Resting in Your loving arms
Trusting in Your sovereignty.

And like the growing Christ child
In wisdom daily learning,
May I ever seek to know You
With my mind and spirit yearning.

Like the Son so faithful
Let me follow in Your light,
Meek and bold, humble and strong
Not afraid to face the night.

Nor cowardly to suffer
And stand for truth alone,
Knowing that Your kingdom
Awaits my going home.

Not afraid to sacrifice
Though great may be the cost,
Mindful how You rescued me
From broken-hearted loss.

Like my risen Savior
The babe, the child, the Son,
May my life forever speak
Of who You are and all You've done.

So while this world rejoices
And celebrates Your birth,
I treasure You, the greatest gift
Unequaled in Your worth.

I long to hear the same words
That welcomed home Your Son,
"Come, good and faithful servant,"
Your Master says, "Well done."

And may heaven welcome others
Who will join with me in praise
Because I lived for Jesus Christ
Not only Christmas Day

General Prayers

120.

Jesus, tender Savior,
You have died for me;
Makes me very thankful
In my heart to Thee.
When the sad, sad story
Of Your grief I read,
Makes me very sorry
For my sins indeed.

Now, I know You live,
And that You plead for me;
Makes me very thankful
In my prayers to Thee.
Soon I hope in heaven
At Your side to stand;
Make me fit to meet You
In that happy land! *Amen.*

121.

Lamb of God, I look to Thee;
You will my example be;
You are gentle, meek, and mild,
You once were a little child.

Ready I would be as You art:
Give me Your obedient heart.
You are humble and kind:
Let me have Your loving mind.

Loving Jesus, gentle Lamb,
In Your gracious hands I am;
Make me, Savior, what You art,
Live Yourself within my heart.

I will then show forth Your praise,
And serve You all my happy days;
Then the world will always see
Christ, the holy Child, in me. *Amen.*

122.

Jesus, help my eyes to see
All the good You send to me.
Jesus, help my ears to hear
Calls for help from far and near.
Jesus, help my feet to go
In the way that You will show.
Jesus, help my hands to do
All things loving, kind, and true.
Jesus, may I helpful be,
Growing every day like Thee. *Amen.*

123.

Come, dearest Savior, take my heart
And let me never from You depart. *Amen.*

124.

Be near me, Lord Jesus!
I ask You to stay
Close by me forever
And love me, I pray.
Bless all the dear children
In Your tender care
And take us all to heaven
To live with You there. *Amen.*

125.

Holy Spirit, give us
Each a lowly mind;
Make us more like Jesus,
Gentle, pure, and kind.

Holy Spirit, brighten
Little deeds of toil,
And our playful pastimes
Let no folly spoil.

Holy Spirit, help us
Daily by Your might
What is wrong to conquer
And to choose what is right. *Amen.*

126.

Jesus, from Your throne on high,
Far above the bright blue sky,
Look on us with loving eye;
Hear us, Lord Jesus!

Be with us every day,
In our work and in our play,
When we learn and when we pray;
Hear us, Lord Jesus!

May we grow from day to day,
Glad to learn each Holy way,
Ever ready to obey;
Hear us, Lord Jesus!

May we ever try to be
From our sinful tempers free,
Pure and gentle, Lord, like Thee;
Hear us, Lord Jesus!

Jesus, Son of God most high,
Who did in the manger lie,
Who upon the cross did die—
Hear us, Lord Jesus! *Amen.*

Special Prayers

For Parents

127.

Almighty and most merciful God, who in Your infinite goodness has given us to our loving parents, who are to watch over us and provide for our needs, we pray Jesus, protect and prolong their life, that we may continue to enjoy their loving care, and strengthen us that as obedient children we may be subject to their will and hold them in love and esteem; through Jesus Christ, our Lord. *Amen.*

For the Teacher

128.

Dear Father in heaven, who in Your goodness has given us teachers that they may instruct and train us in all useful knowledge, we pray our Father, bless them with strength and patience so they may guide our feeble footsteps that, being warned, nurtured, comforted, and strengthened, we may do all things that are pleasing to You and good for us; through Jesus Christ, our Lord. *Amen.*

For the Pastor

129.

Almighty God, who by Your Son Jesus Christ did give to Your holy apostles many excellent gifts and commanded them faithfully to feed Your flock, bless, we ask You, our pastor that he may diligently preach Your holy Word, and grant us the grace to believe Your saving Gospel and to obediently follow the teachings of Your Word, that we may receive the crown of everlasting glory; through Jesus Christ, our Lord. *Amen.*

THE COMMON DOXOLOGY

130.

Praise God, from whom all blessings flow;
Praise Him, all creatures here below;
Praise Him above, ye heavenly host:
Praise Father, Son, and Holy Ghost. *Amen.*

PSALM 23

131.

1. The LORD is my shepherd; I have all that I need.

2. He lets me rest in green meadows; he leads me beside peaceful streams.

3. He renews my strength. He guides me along right paths, bringing honor to his name.

4. Even when I walk through the darkest valley, I will not be afraid, for You are close beside me. Your rod and Your staff protect and comfort me.

5. You prepare a feast for me in the presence of my enemies. You honor me by anointing my head with oil. My cup overflows with blessings.

6. Surely Your goodness and unfailing love will pursue me all the days of my life, and I will live in the house of the LORD forever.

Jesus Loves Me

132.

Jesus loves me!
This I know,
For the Bible tells me so.
Little ones to Him belong;
They are weak but He is strong.

Jesus loves me!
Loves me still,
Tho I'm very weak and ill,
That I might from sin be free,
Bled and died upon the tree.

Jesus loves me!
He who died
Heaven's gate to open wide;
He will wash away my sin,
Let His little child come in.

Jesus loves me!
He will stay
Close beside me all the way.
Thou hast bled and died for me;
I will henceforth live for Thee.

Chorus:
Yes, Jesus loves me!
Yes, Jesus loves me!
Yes, Jesus loves me!
The Bible tells me so.

—*Anna B. Warner, 1820 -1915*

THE LORD'S PRAYER

133.

Our Father who is in heaven; Hallowed be Your Name; Your kingdom come; Your will be done on earth as it is in heaven; Give us today our daily bread; And forgive us our trespasses as we forgive those who trespass against us; And lead us not into temptation; But deliver us from evil; For Yours is the kingdom, and the power, and the glory, forever and ever. *Amen.*